D1576515

2008

A Jewelled Splendour

THE TRADITION OF INDIAN JEWELLERY

A JEWELLED SPLENDOUR

THE TRADITION OF INDIAN JEWELLERY

AshaRani Mathur

Rupa & Co

Published 2002 by

Rupa & Co

7/16, Ansari Road, Daryaganj
New Delhi 110 002

Sales Centres:

Allahabad Bangalore Chandigarh Chennai
Dehradun Hyderabad Jaipur Kathmandu
Kolkata Ludhiana Mumbai Pune

Book Design & Typeset by
Arrt Creations
45 Nehru Apts Kalkaji, New Delhi 110 019

Printed in India by
Ajanta Offset & Packagings

pages 1 and 3: Pendant from an armlet, Benaras, 18th cent. AD
page 2: Kundan and meena-capped emeralds, necklace and earrings, Jaipur
page 5: Jadanagam, South India, 19th cent. AD

CONTENTS

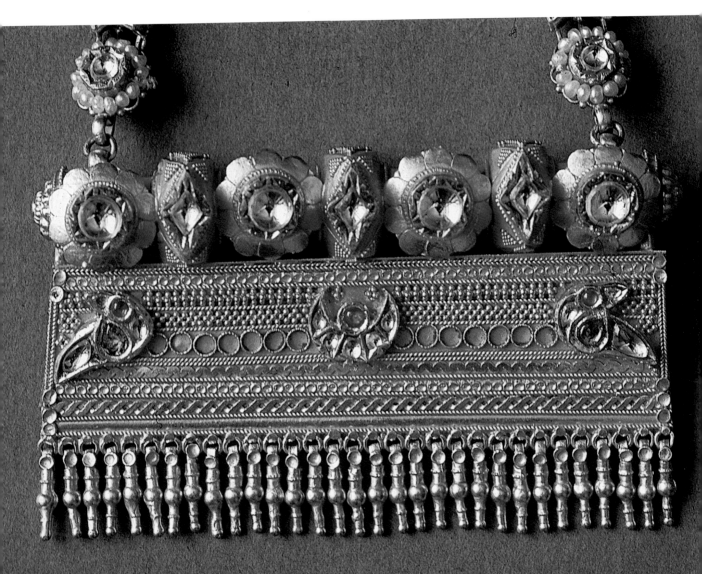

o n e

THE ANCIENT TRADITION

"He had on his left arm a bracelet above the elbow,
which seemed like three rings together,
the middle one larger than the others, all studded with rich jewels,
particularly the middle one, which bore large stones…of very great value."

"Lendas da India", Gaspar Correia, 15th-16th century AD

For centuries the fabled wealth of India, her textiles, her spices, her gold and jewels, attracted traders, invaders, explorers and adventurers. In late medieval times, the earliest armada to land on Indian shores was that of Vasco da Gama, Portuguese soldier of

opp. Tinmaniya (three gems) pendant, Jaipur
The broad, flat pendant bears parrot and moon motifs. Note its fine work, and the continuation of the ancient granulation technique.

fortune, discoverer of the Renaissance route to India. How his eyes must have widened at his first sight of the Zamorin, the ruler of Calicut, blazing with jewellery the like of which he had probably never seen—a gem-studded bracelet with a pendant diamond "the thickness of a thumb"; a gold chain with rubies and an emerald set in its centre; ropes of pearls around his neck, each pearl the size of a hazel nut; his hair swept up into a top knot and adorned with strings of pearls which ended in a large pear-shaped pearl. His ears were pierced to receive many gold earrings, while beside him a page boy stood at the ready with an enormous gold spittoon.

The Zamorin was not alone in his display of fine jewellery whose value was beyond reckoning even in those times. Each ruler, each king, could boast of a similar treasury, some more modest, some infinitely larger, like that of the Emperor of Vijayanagara in whose domain, it was observed, ladies were so heavily laden with jewellery that they had to be supported by other women lest they stagger and fall under their luxurious burden. Many rulers vied with each other to acquire rarer or richer ornaments of exquisite craftsmanship. As well they might. For India was a seemingly inexhaustible source of the finest gold and precious gemstones, an eager consumer herself, a supplier to the rest of the world. What she could not produce, or needed more of, she got from elsewhere, emeralds from Egypt, bullion from Rome.

This love of jewellery permeated all sections of Indian society from the wealthiest to the humblest, as it does to this day; and the fashioning of ornaments was from materials as diverse as precious metals, gemstones, ivory, beads, feathers, cowrie shells, terracotta, berries and animal claws, to name just a few.

opp. Dancing Girl, bronze, Mohenjodaro, Indus Valley, ca. 2500 BC
Perhaps the most famous figure of the Indus Valley civilisation. Her right arm bears two bangles and an armlet, very simple of design, whereas her left arm is covered with bangles. Her necklace has three cowrie shell pendants.

Mother Goddess, late Mauryan, 2nd cent. BC
This depiction is of the Mother Goddess (matrika) as a beautiful young girl. Note the spectacular ornamented head-dress, the necklace and garland, the heavy anklets, and the huge bell-like earring.

But, like most things Indian, there is a resonance beyond the surface. Certainly jewellery was prized as personal adornment, as much for its intrinsic value as for the beauty and precision of its craftsmanship. However its parts and whole held other values far richer than mere monetary worth. Ananda Coomaraswamy's comment on Indian art was equally true of jewellery: it is not just the appearance but the significance that is sought for, not just the object but the concept that stands before it.

opp. Necklace, Harappa, ca. 3000 BC
Recovered from an excavation of an Indus Valley site, this necklace shows an almost contemporary sophistication. The necklace is of steatite and gold beads with pendants of banded agate and jade.

opp. Bangle, Indus Valley, ca. 3000 BC
Made of gold sheet and hollow from the inside, the bangle is a simple wrist adornment.

Necklace, Taxila, 1st cent. AD
A necklace of remarkable charm in Graeco-Roman style, it has gold set with turquoise and garnets. The pendants feature the famed filigree work of Taxila, and its equally famed granulation.

Earrings, Taxila, 1st cent. AD
These earrings, found in an excavation in Sirkap, have a main circle of plain hollowed gold; but notice the fineness of the gold granulation on the pendants, and the clasps in a coil shape.

A world of meaning suffused each piece, each stone, investing it with mysterious powers to act as a talisman to ward off evil or create auspicious and protective auras. Ornamental motifs were symbols of hopes and aspirations; the fish, for example, stood for fertility; curling vines, plants and seeds for fecundity and reproduction. Jewellery and its secret prayer lay on the skin, near the heart or on the forehead, placed on chakras or vital body areas for the greatest efficacy. A woman's ornaments were not just decoration, they brought peace and prosperity to the family and long life to her husband and children.

Not only was jewellery a marker of wealth and status, it identified its wearer in a number of ways, often simultaneously—region, caste, marital status, personal achievements. The cycle of family life was spun out in the rites of passage of its members; each occasion, be it birth or an infant's naming ceremony, the first feeding, the beginning of education, marriage, had its own significant emblems in jewellery. Just as land was immoveable wealth, jewellery was its moveable counterpart, to be added to whenever possible, to be sold only in

opp. Tara, bronze from Kurkihar, 9th cent. AD
The figure of Tara embodies the classical concept of feminine beauty and bears delicately-wrought ornaments. She wears different earrings in either ear, bangles and armlets; a pendanted band adorns her forehead while the lightest of anklets grace her feet.

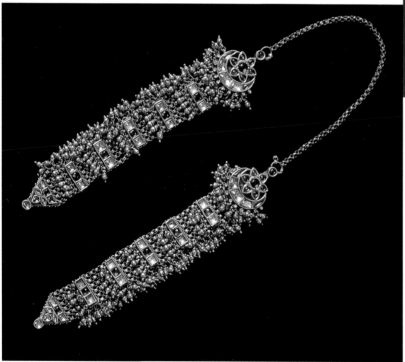

above: Rakhdi, Jaipur
The rakhdi owes its origins to the many head ornaments described in ancient texts. Most were worn on the crest of the head, as was this, never to be seen because they were covered by the head veil. This one has diamonds in a kundan setting of burnished gold.

Jhela with chain, Jaipur
The gold jhela—head ornament—has been carefully crafted to drape over the head and fall to either side of the face, ending in earrings which would have been fixed to the lower ends.

times of distress. It was also streedhan, a
woman's personal wealth, her support
when life inflicted harshness or penury. In
its most perfect form, it was
commissioned and crafted as an act of
piety and devotion to adorn the serene
images of gods in their temples.

Such is the tradition that goes back in an
almost unbroken line for at least 5000 years. We
know this from excavations carried out at the sites of
the Indus Valley civilisations dating back over two millenia
before the Christian era. Here, not only have ornaments been found
but also objects and sculptures, such as the famous Dancing Girl
from Mohenjodaro, which testify to a flourishing tradition. The
finds from the excavated sites show the use of a variety of materials
ranging from gold and silver to faience and an overwhelming array of
beads of semi-precious stones. These were fashioned into bracelets,
bangles, earrings, necklaces and ornaments for the head. Even at that
stage the skill of the craftsman is evident. The goldsmith had moulds
for metal and terra cotta, and he could flatten gold into thin sheets
or mix it with other metals to make alloys. The lapidary could
accomplish the difficult task of boring tiny holes through beads so

that they could be strung into necklaces, bracelets, earrings.

Indeed, it is this genius of the Indian craftsman that has enlivened the jewellery tradition through the centuries. His ability to absorb, his talent for innovation, enabled him to re-fashion and adapt outside influences to create a uniquely Indian fusion. Techniques that originated elsewhere stayed on to become staples of the jeweller's art.

We see this, for example, in the jewellery excavated from Taxila and its environs. Taxila was the old capital of the Gandhara region that lay at the western edge of the Kushan Empire (around 1st century BC to 4th century AD). Later it was Sirkap that became the principal city. Taxila itself had already gone through a chequered history, passing as it did through Greek, Mauryan and other influences before coming under the sway of the Central Asian Kushans. And, since the area stood on the crossroads of a major trade route to the Mediterranean, the influences permeating it had several origins, including Persian and Graeco-Roman. These are visible in the finds from this area comprising necklaces, girdles, pendants, brooches, amulets and earrings.

Lokanatha, gilted bronze from Kurkihar, 11th-12th cent. AD
This striking image of the Bodhisattva Lokanatha is richly bejewelled and detailed in its ornamentation. Note the armlets with their lion heads and the pearl-festooned waistband. A floral motif is delicately repeated throughout.

It was the Greek techniques of granulation and filigree that are seen to such advantage in the Taxila jewellery. Granulation had come to India earlier, probably with Alexander the Great in his attempt to conquer India in the 4th century BC, and there are exceptional examples of this art pre-dating the Taxila finds. In this painstaking process, gold rounds are created through the application of extreme heat that causes the metal to contract into balls or granules. The granules are then sifted to sort out sizes and patterned on a gold surface, being fixed in place through a heating process that requires great skill. In filigree, finely-drawn wires are twisted together and flattened or bent to form designs and motifs. Granulation has been a mainstay since those times, practised even today by goldsmiths from Tamil Nadu to Rajasthan; and perhaps it could be claimed with truth that the exquisite filigree work of Orissa that we see owes its origin to the masters of Taxila.

We have made a jump from the Indus Valley to Taxila, but in the intervening centuries and beyond, much that we know of the jewellery tradition is drawn from other sources. Perhaps this is because of the Indian propensity to re-fashion jewellery by melting down metal and prising out stones. Perhaps, as with deities in bronze, hoards of ornaments were buried deep under the ground as a protection from marauders—who knows? What is certain is that if the vitality of the tradition is not visible through tangible examples, it has at least been preserved for us in sculpture, painting, the great epics, Sanskrit scriptures and literature.

opp. **Hansuli, North India, 18th cent. AD**
The hansuli, a stiff, torque-like necklace, is seen in Kushan sculptures, so clearly it is of ancient origin. This one is richly enamelled and studded with diamonds, rubies and emeralds with a skirting of pearls.

Literary sources provide information about the Vedic period (around 1500 BC). There are references to ornaments in the Rig Veda, a text which abounds in such poetic descriptions as karna-shobhana for the adornment of the ear. But it is not until later, when we come to the great sculptures of the Mauryans, the Shungas, the Shatavahanas and the Kushans, that we are able to actually see the words come to life. It is a grand parade of figures that we encounter, gods and kings and queens, saints and sinners, beautiful nymphs and inebriated harlots. Except for those deliberately left austere, they are draped one and all with jewellery from forehead to ankle. Their necks are adorned with a profusion of chokers, chains, pearl strands, their arms encased from forearm to wrist, their waists and hips girdled. The monuments at Bharhut, Sanchi and Amaravati, the images from

Gandhara and Mathura, all bear witness to a spectacular and vital tradition, the unknown sculptors capturing with grace and precision the art of the jeweller.

Far to the south, discoveries in Tamil Nadu yielded a rich hoard of coins and jewellery dating as far back as the 1st century BC, a time when direct trade between India and Rome flourished. The gold jewellery includes rings and a pendant, reminders of an era when poets sang of the Yavana seamen who came to the wealthy ports of the southern shores bearing gold. Gold was used in abundance in the south as jewellery offered to gods and worn by kings alike. The Chola kings were generous in their endowments to temples, and inscriptions list the details of the jewellery that poured out from the royal treasury to adorn images of the deities. No less than 65 different ornaments featured on the vast repertoire of the Chola jewellers, from necklaces of various kinds to bejewelled waistbands.

This was all of a piece with the fascination for jewellery displayed in the epics and literature. In the Ramayana, as the abducted Sita is forced to go to Lanka with the demon Ravana, she drops her jewelled armband and earrings to indicate the path she has taken.

opp. Mukut, ca. 19th cent. AD, Jaipur
The mukut, a crown-like head ornament, is mentioned in Sanskrit texts. Here, set in kundan and rubies, it has been inverted as a necklace, with two delicate pendants fringed with Basra pearls.

Nath, nose-ring, Himachal Pradesh, 19th cent. AD
The nath or nose-ring though not part of the ancient Indian repertoire has now become a staple. The gold here is studded with gems and pearls. At the upper end, the foliage is embellished with stones, while below tiny gold leaves shimmer in the light.

In the Mahabharata, the valiant Karna, scion of the Sun God, is born with divine armour and earrings that render him invincible. But when, in a fateful gesture, he is tricked into cutting them off, he is doomed to die. In the immortal Shakuntala of Kalidasa, the eponymous heroine is abandoned by her royal husband until the ring he has given her comes to light and his memory returns. In the great Tamil poem of the Sangam age, Silappadikaram, a man is condemned to death after being falsely accused of having stolen a jewelled anklet from the queen. His wife's grief turns to fury, and the intensity of her rage sets a whole city on fire.

Karnaphool and jhumka, Jaipur, ca. 19th cent. AD
Pair of karnaphools (floral studs for the ears) with hanging jhumkas. White sapphires, Basra pearls and fine Jaipur enamelling feature in this pair, probably commissioned for a buyer from Lucknow.

THE ANCIENT TRADITION

Rounded breasts adorned with gems sandal-scented,
Broad curving hips with girdle bands all belled,
Sweet-sounding anklets making music on delicate feet,
So do women enhance their beauty…

Kalidas, from Ritusamharam, The Seasons

In the familiar and much-loved stories described above, jewellery plays a dramatic and central role. But on a softer and much more romantic note, it is the essential accoutrement of a seductive maiden whose anklets jingle enticingly as she walks. It is part of the solah shringar enjoined by ancient texts, the sixteen artful decorations used by a woman to make herself beautiful for her beloved. There on that list, amidst the scented baths, hair oils, fragrant unguents and henna, lie the essentials of jewellery, no less than eight separate items. Among them were the kundala or earrings, celebrated in folklore as love's messengers. The mala, or necklace, was to be placed around a swan-like neck; pre-eminent among the many kinds of necklaces was the mangalsutra, the tali of South India. It was and remains the sacred symbol of marriage from which a woman would never part unless she had to. There were bangles and anklets and karadarpana, the mirrored ring that permitted a quick glance at her own beauty.

Jewellery, however, was not a feminine preserve. Men revelled in it as well, decorating their persons, their tools of work, whether they be weapons and shields or studded covers for the horns of animals. Each region had its stylistic variations or distinctions, and in the nuanced vocabulary of Sanskrit there were precise names for each piece identifying the design, the purpose and the significance. For pearl necklaces alone there was a plethora of names, the induchhanda for that with 1008 strings, the vijayachhanda for that with 504. So specific were the names that the original meaning of balika was an ear ornament "formed of three pearls comparable to the bakul flower".

Armlet, Rajasthan, 19th cent. AD
A decorative and ornamental armlet with kundan gold work inset with diamonds. Note the brilliant red enamel so characteristic of Jaipur whose enamellers held the secret of its rich ruby colour.

From top to toe, both men and women adorned themselves with a dazzling array of jewellery as we see from the sculptures and paintings of the Gupta period and onwards. The head was decorated with the chudamani or crest jewel, the mukut or crown; the forehead with the tika that hung in the centre or with jewelled strips along the hairline. It was inauspicious to leave them naked, thus the profusion of jewellery for the ears—plugs, studs, hoops, graceful hanging jhumkas. The neck bore chokers, chains, collars, ropes of pearls and beads whereas armlets, bangles and bracelets covered upper and lower arms. Waists and hips, ample or sinous, carried belts and girdles made of gold or silver studded with stones; these could be rigid, flexible, braided or highly ornamented. Anklets graced the feet, almost always of silver, for to wear gold on the feet was to profane its deity, Lakshmi, Goddess of Wealth. Only royalty considered themselves exempt from this observance.

From north to south, east to west, the great temples and sculptures of Bharhut, Sanchi, Belur and Halebid, Thanjavur, Orissa, Khajuraho, to name just a few, spread over time and under the influences of various dynasties, display this stunning wealth of the jeweller's art.

METAL AND STONE

"Gold is the seed of Agni, God of Fire…"

the Satapatha Brahmana

Of all the material used in Indian jewellery, no other is quite as magnificent a national obsession as gold. Consider the facts. India holds close to one-third of the world's gold, the bulk of which is in private hands in the form of jewellery. The subcontinent has been an insatiable consumer of gold since recorded history, drawing the metal from its own mines and supplementing that with imports

opp. Carved and studded emerald pendant, Jaipur
The Mughals were especially fond of emeralds and embellished them with inscriptions and carving. This magnificent Colombian emerald is studded with a kundan-set diamond in the centre and surrounded by round cut diamonds.

Granulated gold bangles, Jodhpur
The traditional name for these bangles is gajra.
Fine gold wires hold gold grains in place so evenly that all the curves are identical.

of bullion since Roman times. When at last the mines were played out, India continued to buy gold from elsewhere and remains to this day by far the largest buyer of the precious metal. India leads in not just consumption but fabrication as well. Once used to fashion coins as well as jewellery, and drawn out into fine thread for weaving sumptuous brocades, gold is now largely used for ornaments. It is estimated that there are about 100,000 workshops of varying sizes across the country where goldsmiths work their magic to create new jewellery or re-make old family jewellery into new designs.

What explains this fascination for gold? It has its origins in ancient beliefs. The giver of gold, says the Rig Veda, receives a life of light and glory. Gold was called hiranya, from the Sanskrit root hri meaning imperishable; the Hiranyagarbha or Golden Womb is the source of all Creation manifest in the radiant form of Brahma Himself. In Ayurveda, the vital chakra of the heart is depicted as golden-yellow in colour, an inspiration to divine thoughts. Within the lustrous metal is held the warmth of the sun, giver of life and food. Gold is associated with prosperity, more specifically with Lakshmi, Goddess of Wealth, whose auspicious benedictions are invoked with the giving and receiving of gold. That is why it plays such an important part in the festival of Diwali dedicated to the Goddess, where the purchase of at least one gold ornament is considered mandatory. The great epics, mythology and literature are full of references to gold; and Chanakya's Arthashastra, a text dating back to Mauryan times (around 4th century BC) details the rules to be observed by goldsmiths and the various alloys that they may make from it.

Perhaps much of the fascination with gold has to do with its intrinsic properties. Its inherent value makes it one of the most liquid of investments. Rightly did the seers call it imperishable, for it neither corrodes nor rusts; gold artefacts excavated at ancient sites have been found as bright and shiny as the day they were made. So soft and malleable is it that a single gram can be drawn out into a fine wire three and a half kilometres in length; or a single ounce can be hammered into a sheet of 16 square metres!

This very softness makes it difficult to work in its purest form, 24 karat, since the surface can be easily scratched; that is why it is most often used in some form of alloy to harden the metal. In India the most desired is 22 karat, which has a gold content of over 90%. Alloys are formed with different metals, such as silver, copper, nickel and platinum; and varying combinations of these metals lead to different purities, and colours such as green gold, white gold, yellow gold and rose gold. Since traditionally in India most people prefer the colour to remain as close as possible to that of pure gold, jewellery has usually been made of yellow gold alloys.

On this basic material the goldsmith and his workers have created a variety of effects, etching, hammering, engraving, hatching, embossing and faceting the metal to bring out its lustrous versatility. The softest gold is used to encase gemstones in the kundan technique, which is detailed later in the book. We have already touched upon the fineness of granulation and filigree, but one of the most remarkable and skilful techniques was that of enamelling, still a perfected art in India, which too we shall see later.

All these techniques were brought to bear on bridal jewellery, of which gold forms an essential part in almost all regions of India, though the repertoire varies from one area to another. Across the country, the most basic ornaments—preferably in 22 karat gold—would be a necklace, earrings, a pair of bangles and a ring; the wealthier the family, the larger the amount and value of the jewellery given.

Necklace pendant box, Jaipur
The pendant bears exquisite gold work and is centred with a carved emerald.

If gold evoked the brightness of the sun, silver was its feminine counterpart, steeped in the cool luminosity of the moon. For thousands of years silver was believed to have magical and healing properties. An ancient discovery that the purity of water, milk and vinegar could be preserved for longer periods in silver vessels led to the metal being used as a container on long voyages. Indeed, what are said to be the largest silver vessels in the world now stand in the City Palace Museum in Jaipur; they were used by a 19th century monarch to transport the sacred waters of the Ganga across the seas to England.

Like gold, in its purest form silver (or fine silver, as it is

called) is too soft to be properly worked and is combined with
another metal, usually copper, to render it harder and more durable.
In India, any silver jewellery has at least 50% purity, or else it
cannot be truly called silver, and probably nobody would buy it.
How the alloy is proportioned differs from one state to the other;
for example, ornaments in Gujarat consist of 70% silver, whereas in
adjoining Rajasthan, a higher percentage is the norm.

Whatever the proportion, silver jewellery has a vigour and liveliness
all its own, many of its designs preserving an antique originality. If
gold was the preferred metal of the affluent, silver was the staple of
the rural and tribal areas. It was a means of saving money, and an
indication of a person's wealth. The jewellery was a mobile "bank",
serving as both adornment to be kept on the person and a stand-by
in times of need. This is perhaps one reason why the jewellery
appears so heavy and chunky.

opp. Hansuli, from the Lambadis of Andhra Pradesh
The silver hansuli or necklace is a sign
of marriage amongst the women of the
tribe. The triangular danglers indicate
that she has borne sons.

Silver armlet, probably Andhra Pradesh, early 20th cent. AD
Probably from the Sugali or Lambadi
tribe, the intricate cast silver work is
set in cotton threads looped at one end to
tighten the ornament around the forearm.

Areas, and communities within areas, had their own distinctive design vocabularies, and local silversmiths fashioned the metal into beaded chokers, long ropes of chains, heavy collars, pendant boxes, a huge variety of bangles, bracelets, wristlets and amulets, nose rings and, of course, anklets. Of anklets alone, there is an almost bewildering range which seems to go from heavy to heaviest! So large are some anklets that you would think they make walking impossible; but they are lighter than they look, being hollow within. In hill areas, silver was studded with semi-precious stones like turquoise, coral or agate. And in the drylands of Banni in Kutch, the dun landscape is like a backdrop for some of the most spectacular jewellery in India. Here, as elsewhere, the jewellery, the clothes, the embroideries, are all social identifiers, indicating where the woman is from, to what caste she belongs and whether she is married.

It is the jewels that are bedecked by women,
Not women who are beautified by them:
A woman unbejewelled will still enrapture,
But who looks twice at any girl-less gem?

Sanskrit, from the Paddhati of Sharngadhara

The irony of this poem may make you smile, but—contrary to the poet's belief—it is a fact that gems exert a strange magnetic pull. Jewellery exhibitions the world over attract audiences who do indeed look twice at "girl-less gems", as much for their beauty and flawlessness as for their rarity and thus value.

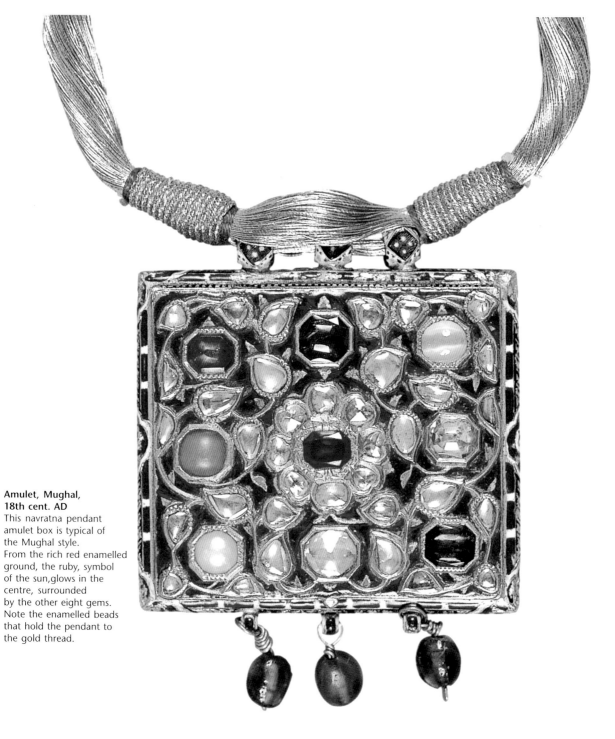

Amulet, Mughal, 18th cent. AD
This navratna pendant amulet box is typical of the Mughal style.
From the rich red enamelled ground, the ruby, symbol of the sun, glows in the centre, surrounded by the other eight gems. Note the enamelled beads that hold the pendant to the gold thread.

And yet what are gems after all but stones of greater or lesser antiquity mined from the earth or drawn from the sea? What makes them so treasured is the extraordinary emotional connotations, the magic powers, we invest in them. They are the talismans of our fortunes, our connection to the cosmos, bringers of luck and prosperity, twined with our very existence through the auspiciousness of birthstones.

In India gemstones have always had a special place in both religious and secular life. They were used for ritual and sacramental purposes, they represented protection against malevolent forces, and had healing powers. Beyond their monetary worth, which in many cases was considerable, they held cosmic and spiritual attributes. Little wonder, then, that there were a number of ancient Sanskrit texts devoted to the study of this subject, works like Ratnapariksha, Mani Mala, Brhat Samhita, the Garuda Purana.

A description in the Garuda Purana ascribes the origin of gemstones to the slaying of the demon, Vala, whose severed limbs were transformed into precious gem seeds. As the demigods jostled for the seeds, some fell to earth, scattering over the seas, rivers, mountains and forests. The seeds germinated into lodes of gemstones; Vala's blood was dropped by Surya the Sun God into the "deep pools of Bharata" where it transmuted into beautiful rubies of wonderful colour and brilliance. His teeth "fell like stars into the oceans

opp. Navratna necklace, Jaipur
In this delicate example, we see an almost miniaturised version of the nine jewels theme. Fringed with Basra pearls, the gemstones appear in the prescribed order: the ruby as the sun in the centre surrounded by other stones representing the heavenly bodies visualised in relation to the sun.

below" and became seeds for gems with the lustre of moonbeams: pearls. And so on…until the demon's entire body was transformed into the seeds for diamonds, emeralds, coral, topaz, cat's eyes, sapphires, zircons. Each stone acquired its own powers and characteristics. Together, they became the fabled navaratna, the nine jewels which, when worn in combination, acted as a talisman for the wearer and possessed healing energies.

The belief in the potency of the navaratna was linked to the colours of the spectrum, the chakras or nodal points of the body and the planets. Our universe vibrates with cosmic energies, says the ancient tradition of Ayurveda, and there exists a relationship between these forces and colours, metals, gems and humans. Gems possess astral powers, they are the prisms for cosmic light and their colours serve to concentrate that energy in the human body. Each of the nine gems is connected with a colour; each with a planet, the sun and the moon; and their healing powers manifest as they radiate through the chakras to revitalise the body. Not only can gems enhance benevolent planetary influences, they can also protect against malevolent ones. The overall effect is one of harmony of mind and body, charging the wearer with positive energies, bringing him good fortune and protecting him from harm.

On each item of jewellery where they feature, the nine gems are arranged in an allegory of the cosmos. At the heart or in the centre lies the ruby, the powerful sun, in relation to whom all other heavenly bodies are perceived as placed in cardinal or intermediary points. Ranged around or across are diamond (Venus, east), pearl (moon, south-east), emerald (Mercury, north-east), blue sapphire (Saturn, west), yellow sapphire or topaz (Jupiter, north-west), zircon (Rahu, the ascending node of the moon, south-west), cat's eye (Ketu, the descending node of the moon, north), and finally, coral (Mars, south). Each gem possessed characteristic powers of enhancing or controlling individual traits or suppressing undesirable ones: emeralds, for example, had positive influences on intellect and wit, whereas diamonds were associated with inner and outer refinement. Blue sapphires, though, had to be used with

Necklace, Hyderabad, ca. 19th cent. AD
An exceptionally fine example of Hyderabadi meena or enamelling. Both sides of the necklace can be seen; the delicate motifs are those of a bud of the champa flower, seen on white sapphires on the obverse whereas the reverse, in green meena, is alive with champa flowers in full bloom.

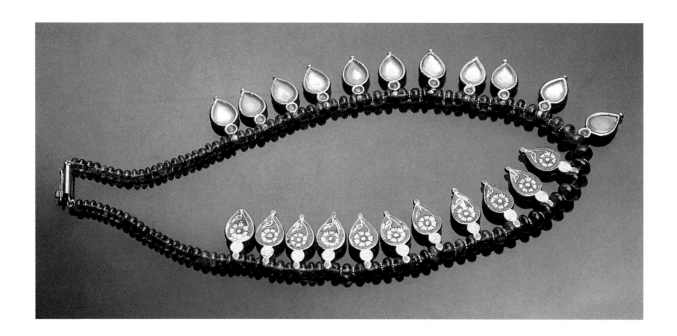

Diamond
Diamonds are carbons crystallized under extreme temperatures and pressures for millions of years, thus creating the hardest known natural substance. Because it is composed of a single element, it is also the purest of gemstones.

caution and under supervision for the influence of Saturn could often prove obstructive; and it was only when the gemstone was combined in a particular manner with respect to the individual that its beneficent effects were felt.

Ayurveda also uses gems for medicinal purposes, reducing the stones to powder (pishti) or ashes (bhasma) to extract their therapeutic qualities. Ground in a pestle and mortar, they are made into smooth pastes with the addition of rose or kewra water as cures for a vast number of diseases and ailments. Thus administered, blue sapphire was said to cure epilepsy, and pearl to relieve calcium deficiencies. Ruby, in powder and ash form, was said to improve blood circulation, whereas emerald was efficacious for heart diseases. Diamonds, however, were never made into powder, only ashes; perhaps this was because it could be dangerous, fatal even, for a piece of the gem to slip into the stomach.

With the moonstone beauty of her face,
Her sapphire-black tresses,
Her hands the ruby of red lotuses,
She glowed with the magic of gems

Sanskrit, poem by Bhartrihari

Diamond Ring
Diamonds are forever...a symbol of the eternity of love. Its unique ability to reflect light gives the diamond its dazzle. But much depends also on the cut of the stone; clarity, colour and carats are the other factors which lead to a stone's valuation.

Of the nine gems of the navaratna, five are considered as the Maharatnani or "greater" gems; these are diamonds, rubies, emeralds, sapphires and pearls.

Perhaps no jewel exerts as much fascination as a diamond, the purest and hardest of gemstones. Look into its heart and see an infinite luminous pool; its unique ability to reflect light made the ancients believe that it was part of a hardened dewdrop or frozen lightning. In India, various colours of the stone were associated with different deities, yellow with Indra, the God of the Heavens; brown with the God of Fire, Agni; copper with the Maruts, Lords of the Storms; green with Vishnu the Preserver.

Diamond pendant, obverse (above) and reverse (left), Jaipur
A splendid kundan-set diamond in the obverse; on the reverse is finely-wrought enamel simulation inlay with soft gold and gemstones, emeralds, rubies and diamonds. Such precise hand-cutting and setting was a Mughal speciality, as was the typical floral motif.

opp. Rubelite pendant, Jaipur
Necklace pendant with a Quranic verse inscribed on the rubelite stone, which is delicately surrounded by uncut diamonds set in kundan.

Diamonds were first mined in India at least 3000 years ago. Until the 18th century, India was the only known source for the stone, believed to come from the legendary mines of Golconda, although in actual fact the gems originated from a number of other mines in the Deccan; Golconda was the prime trading area. Whatever their actual source, the "Golconda" diamonds were a benchmark for purity, clarity and size. Some of the world's largest and most famous stones came from here, such as the Koh-i-noor, the Mountain of Light—now in the British Crown jewels—surely the most legendary of all diamonds. Then there is the Darya-e-noor, Sea of Light, a dazzling pink stone which was looted by the Persian invader Nadir Shah, and the sapphire-blue Hope diamond. The Babur diamond, appropriated after his victory at the Battle of Panipat, was so huge that its value was said to amount to the cost of two and a half day's food for the entire world! Then there is the Orlov diamond, whose whereabouts are not known today, said to be abstracted from the deity of the Srirangam temple and sold to Catherine the Great of Russia.

The mines are all but gone now, victims of utter depletion and the discovery of diamonds elsewhere in the world, but the connection with the diamond trade remains by way of an entire industry based on cutting and polishing stones. Eight out of ten smaller diamonds sold worldwide are cut and polished in India by an estimated workforce of 800,000, mainly in the states of Gujarat, Rajasthan and Maharashtra, among others.

Ruby has the rich red warmth of the sun, with which it is associated; indeed, the best rubies were those which held at their heart the deepest, truest red like "the colour of a drop of blood / Shed on the white neck of a wounded dove"... Their origin was the fabled mines of Pegu in Burma, today's Myanmar, and entire communities of merchants, such as the Chettiars of Tamil Nadu, made their fortunes from trading in this stone. Alike in colour, but not the same, is the red spinel, a stone often used as a bead.

Ruby necklace, Jaipur
Ruby inlaid necklace with gold work, Jaipur

Sapphire is the gem of the heavens, cherished for thousands of years. The ancient Persians believed that the earth lay upon a giant sapphire whose reflection was the azure sky. The most valuable sapphires are a deep velvety blue, such as the mayur neelam or peacock blue of the stones that used to be obtained from Kashmir. A far earlier source was Sri Lanka whose stones are still prized for the range of beautiful colours from sky blue to a deep midnight. Blue is not the only colour of the sapphire, however; the so-called "fancy sapphires" are seen in shades of purple, green, yellow and smoky brown.

Sapphire and diamond kada, Jaipur
Sapphires of many colours—called "fancy sapphires"—adorn this bracelet; in between are diamonds in floral patterns.

"Emeralds of dark green colour,
or the colour of a spring meadow; of a soft glow...
hewn in different ways...endowed with qualities of shape, which
shoot diffusions of light
when the sun's rays fall on it..."

from the Garuda Purana

The emerald, gem of eternal spring, was a great favourite of the Mughals. Its use in India is of far greater antiquity, however, since it is mentioned in the Rig Veda and in the epic, the Mahabharata. The earliest source was Egypt whose mines lay near Aswan and who for centuries held a monopoly over the gemstone. That monopoly was broken with the Spanish conquest of what is now Colombia; from the 16th century onwards Colombian emeralds were sold to the wealthy of India, the rulers and their nobility.

Pearl, cooling gem of the moon, is the most widely and lavishly used gemstone in the tradition of Indian jewellery. There were two early sources, the Persian Gulf around Bahrain which yielded the famous Basra pearls, and the Indian fisheries in the Gulf of Mannar. Pearls were a popular and important item of trade, though the best gems remained in the hands of the rulers who controlled the fisheries and the trade.

It was the same with other gemstones. The locations of the mines were kept strictly secret and access to them severely restricted. The choicest stones were the prerogative of the ruler, but this was not a function of greed alone. To have a treasure chest of gems and jewellery gave rulers power of two kinds, temporal power for conquests and supremacy, and the spiritual and psychic fortunes conveyed by the inherent cosmic potency of the gems. They probably believed staunchly in the precept of the Agni Purana which said that a gem free of all impurities and radiating its characteristic lustre was to be considered the harbinger of good luck.

opp. & right: Emerald pendant, sarpech motif, Jaipur
A central carved emerald and three perfectly matched drops catch our attention in this pendant of Mughal design, shaped like the sarpech or turban ornament. On the obverse (left) the diamonds are cut; on the reverse (right) leaves and flowers are depicted in green enamel.

THE GREAT TRADITION: NORTH AND SOUTH

"In jewells (which is one of his felicityes)
hee is the treasury of the world,
buyeing all that comes, and heaping rich stones
as if hee would rather build then weare them."

Sir Thomas Roe about the Emperor Jehangir, 17th century AD

Even in a country long reknown for its jewellery tradition, the Mughal Emperors set a new benchmark in techniques and elegance. The dynasty represented a watershed in jewellery aesthetics, spurring craftsmen to greater heights with the

opp. Jadeite pendant, Jaipur
The sea-green jadeite is a perfect foil for the delicate gold wire inlay studded with rubies and diamonds in a floral motif. Notice how precise and clean cut the work is.

discernment of their demands, adopting with enthusiasm motifs from India such as the nine stones of the navaratna, lavishly displayed in necklaces and armlets. It was not jewellery alone that engaged their artistic attention. With their arrival, the colour palette of textiles changed, softened, to absorb the pastel shades born of a more temperate climate. Architecture took a new turn, the squat dome of the Afghans replaced by the ethereal double dome of the Persians. The Mughal genius was to bring new ideas to the craftsmen of Hindustan while building upon their inherent skills. In many ways it was beauty both redefined and refined, rising to heights of excellence rarely surpassed in succeeding centuries. At the pinnacle of empire, they achieved a synthesis of Islamic style and Indian workmanship that astounded the rest of the world.

We see jewellery everywhere: in the delicate patkas or waistbands crafted from fine muslins, in the glowing colours of the miniature paintings commissioned for portfolios, in the monumental marble inlaid with semi-precious stones, on almost any stone or metal surface. The adornment of surfaces was a Mughal métier and articles of everyday use, from pen stands to wine cups to huqqa bases and dagger hilts, were richly patterned with gold inlay and precious stones. The decorative impulse was born of the taste that Babur brought with him from the grasslands of the Ferghana, nourished by Persian influences, brought to fruition by Indian hands.

All this was not without its practical side. It was the Mughal show of strength, a means of quelling potential rebellion through a display of the sheer dazzling opulence that represented

opp. Nayika, miniature painting from Deogarh, 18th cent. AD
The gracefully arched body of the maiden shows off her jewellery. Forearms, wrists, neck and ankles are lavishly ornamented. Her hands bear the hath-phool and the jhoomar in her hair seems to sway as enticingly as the girdle across her hips.

Hath-phool, Northern India, 19th cent. AD
The hath-phool (literally, hand flower) was an elaborate ornament comprising a wristlet and a decorated motif for the back of the hand, and culminating in rings for the fingers. The ornament pictured here is worked in gold studded with rubies, diamonds and emeralds and a border of pearls.

opp. Bangle, Rajasthan,
19th cent. AD
In this classic combination of
enamels and gems, the bangle
(one of a pair) has part of its outer
surface set with diamonds and
rubies. The front is frilled with
seed pearls held on gold wire,
whereas the inner surface is rich
with red and green enamelling on
a white base.

Lady being offered wine,
miniature painting from
Golconda, Deccan,
17th cent. AD
Here, the jewellery appears all the
more luxuriant for being placed
against the boldly-striped sari.
There is a lavish use of pearls so
favoured in the Deccan, but there
is also an intricate gold girdle
below the waistband. The anklets
are delicate, and on the foot,
marked with red alta, we can
glimpse the toe-ring.

power. It was a statement of empire by a dynasty that carried the bitter race memory of struggle and failure. Jewellery and gemstones were the easily portable materials that powered conquest or were stand-bys in times of need. In the 16th century, the beleaguered Humayun sought shelter at the court of Shah Tahmasp of Persia; in return he had to hand as tribute the Babur diamond which his father had taken from Ibrahim Lodi after the Battle of Panipat. (Some believe that the gem given was the Koh-i-noor; others, that in fact the two are one and the same stone.)

No wonder, then, that the collection of such riches was important. Gems and jewellery, indeed whole mines, were the tributes exacted from loyal subjects and vassals. They enhanced the treasury vastly, as did the estates of dead nobles and heirless families.

The Mughals also loved jewellery and gemstones as intrinsic objects of beauty and had an obssession for gathering the finest. An ever-meticulous monarch, Akbar established karkhanas or workshops for various disciplines in his City of Victory at Fatehpur Sikri. Here, in addition to the crafting of jewellery, he entrusted the buying and selling of gems to four officials who

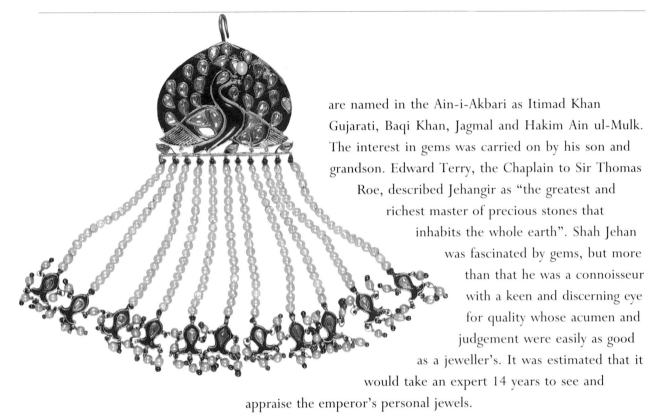

are named in the Ain-i-Akbari as Itimad Khan Gujarati, Baqi Khan, Jagmal and Hakim Ain ul-Mulk. The interest in gems was carried on by his son and grandson. Edward Terry, the Chaplain to Sir Thomas Roe, described Jehangir as "the greatest and richest master of precious stones that inhabits the whole earth". Shah Jehan was fascinated by gems, but more than that he was a connoisseur with a keen and discerning eye for quality whose acumen and judgement were easily as good as a jeweller's. It was estimated that it would take an expert 14 years to see and appraise the emperor's personal jewels.

Jhoomar, North India, probably Mughal, 18th cent. AD
The jhoomar is worn on one side of the forehead or above the ear. Above is a sumptuous combination of enamel, diamonds and pearls. A brilliant blue peacock rises from the rich green ground, while below, strings of pearls end in a row of finely-wrought enamelled little fish, emblems of fertility. The peacock holds a pearl in his beak, the most delicate of poetic jewelled conceits.

How eerily reminiscent of the Vijayanagara empire to the south. Here too there was a richness of gems, available in the bazaars with the same ease as flowers or cloth. On auspicious festival nights, the Raya's wives would march in a procession bearing golden lamps, each so weighed down by gem-encrusted robes and her own jewellery that she could scarcely walk. When the empire was defeated at the Battle of Talikota, it took the victorious armies nearly six months to strip the city of its riches and reduce it to rubble.

Two centuries later and far to the north a similar event occurred with the sacking of Delhi by Nadir Shah. It took him a fortnight just to melt down the Mughal gold and silver. Thousands of chests of metals, gems and jewellery left the country, including the famous Peacock Throne.

Yet there remains a living heritage, not just the objects and artefacts seen in museums but in the fine techniques practised even today and a vocabulary of exquisite jewellery motifs. One of the most enduring parts of this legacy is the technique of enamelling, which was perhaps not new to India but which rose under the Mughals to a high point of refinement.

Bangles, Benaras, Mughal, 19th cent. AD
Elephant trunks intertwine in this pair of bangles wrought in Benaras in its famous gulabi-meena or rose-coloured enamel. The bracelets are set in diamonds, and rose and green enamel work with floral motifs decorates the insides of the bracelets.

Jhoomar, Jaipur
Worn on the side of the head, we may imagine this ornament emerging from under the head veil of a shy bride. Only the end piece would have been visible, and this is richly ornamented on both sides, on the obverse with kundan and pearls, on the reverse with delicate bird, floral and foliate motifs in red, white and green enamel.

But before we come to enamelling, let us look at kundan which provides the field, as it were. Kundan is a technique used for setting stones. The purest, softest gold is hammered into very fine sheets and literally moulded around the stones to encase them and hold them in place. The stones can then be cut or polished as the design demands. Because the stones are encased, the light strikes them only from above; so, to provide depth and refraction, a piece of foil— gold, silver or coloured—is placed under the stone to give it a glow. Kundan—practised in this form only in India—has several advantages over Western-style bezel or claw setting. Most importantly, it eliminates the time and labour needed to fabricate each setting separately to the size of the stone thus giving the craftsman the freedom to use irregular shapes and sizes. In turn, this means that a stone need only be minimally cut, preserving as far as possible its original size. And it enables work to be carried out without soldering or applying heat, since the gold is soft enough to encase the stone by simply pressing it in.

Kundan setting with exquisite enamelling on the reverse was a great favourite of the Mughals and remains one of the most prized forms of the jewellery repertoire even today.

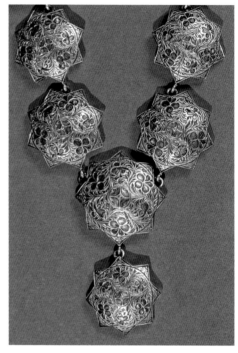

Reverse of a necklace, Jaipur
The styling of the reverse is reminiscent of an old Mughal method of decorative engraving. Here, however, we are able to see clearly the technique of meena engraving and what the ground must have looked like before the colours or enamels were applied.

Adiya ("of the rich") necklace, Jaipur
One of the most lavish examples of the jeweller's repertoire, the adiya necklace features a rigid choker from which flows a cascade of set gems. In this fine example, we see the kundan work and brilliant red enamel of Jaipur.

The enamelling process itself demands the pooling of a number of skills and so an entire team of specialists works on a single piece. First, the designer selects a design which is then passed to the goldsmith. He in turn creates the appropriate gold form and gives it back to the designer who now outlines the pattern on the surface and burnishes it so that the pattern stands out. It is then the engraver's turn to work on the piece, which calls for great skill and precision as the jewellery surfaces are small. Most Indian enamelling is of the kind called champleve, literally, raised field, so the engraver's task is to excavate those areas of the metal that will take the enamel by carving them out. These lowered surfaces are hatched with fine parallel lines to enable a thorough fusion between colour and metal; this adds to the visual delight as the hatchings enhance the play of light and shade over the transparent colours.

The next stage is undertaken by the meenakar or enameller who will fill in the colours to the level of the surface (raising the field) and then fuse them to the gold through repeated firings. Since the enamels are of various hardness and thus require different temperatures for fusing, they must be fired separately and in a particular sequence that goes from hardest (highest temperature) to softest (lowest temperature). Cooling is as important as heating; a flaw at this stage could crack the enamel or render it undesirably opaque. The usual colour sequence begins with white and runs through blue, green, black and yellow before reaching red. Rich ruby is the signature colour of Jaipur enamelling and achieves here an unmatched brilliance and clarity. "The purer the gold, the richer the colour," goes an old saying, and the red meena of Jaipur is applied to a high karat gold.

Kalgi pendant earrings, Jaipur
The pendants are shaped like the kalgi, the jewelled feather set in turbans. Kundan is fringed with spinels; there are Basra pearls including on the part that hooks the ornament to the hair. The reverse is enamelled.

Necklace, Mughal, 18th cent. AD
A stunning Navratna necklace of the
Mughal style. Plaques are studded
with precious and semi-precious stones,
including the nine auspicious gems,
and strung together. Pearls embellish the
upper part of the necklace, whose back is
enamelled with birds and floral motifs.

**opp. Sarpech, turban ornament,
Mughal, 18th cent. AD**
Turbans were embellished with sarpatti,
or a forehead band, and a jewelled plume.
In this lavish example of the Mughal style,
a large hexagonal carved emerald
dominates the centre, with two smaller
rectangular emeralds at the sides.
Large uncut emeralds hang below and
at the tip of the plume, while diamonds are
set all around.

We are not finished yet. For now the enamelled surfaces must be
polished so that they lie evenly with the rest of the surface. The
jewellery then goes to the kundan setter before being sent to the
patua or stringer, whose task is to thread the jewellery with
drawstrings and make it ready to wear.

Given the sometimes minute surfaces that are worked on, the wealth
of detail and depth of colour are truly amazing. This is jewellery at
its most precise yet ornamental, where elaborate vines curl around
flowers and birds dance in monsoon delight. Why then is some
enamelling only at the back of the jewellery, where it cannot be
seen at all? There are many answers, some practical, some more

complex. High karat gold had to be protected from the wear and tear of use; such protection was given by the enamelled surface which also stiffened the gold and retained its shape. But some theorists believe in pehchan, that secret recognition that exists between the maker and the wearer, which needs no public approbation to validate it. It is a form of artistic tryst, an unspoken bond between the educated appreciation of the buyer and the finely-honed skills of the craftsman. As a concept, it has an elegance and sophistication equal to that of the art itself.

Enamelling, however, was not the only contribution of the Mughals. Their love of emeralds brought the gemstone into wide use during this era. Green is, of course, the colour associated with Islam; in the Sufi belief, an emerald mountain stands for the highest level of spiritual aspiration. The stones were used in a number of ways, and often worked upon by master lapidaries who carved motifs of flowers or foliage on them or inscribed them with

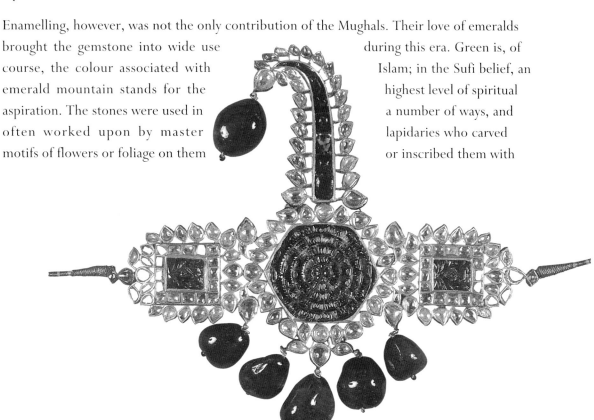

opp. Rudraksha mala, Tamil Nadu, 19th cent. AD
In the wealthy mercantile community of the Nattukotai Chettiars men's necklaces like the one pictured here, combining the sacred rudraksha beads with finely-wrought gold, are worn for festive occasions such as the 60th birthday. The necklace has a casket, above which is a figure of Nataraja poised in dance.

Tourmaline ring, Jaipur
In this deep rose tourmaline ring, two inscriptions are visible: one, a sacred Islamic text, the other, the floral motif, both in gold.

sacred words. To inscribe lineage on a gemstone was a means of its perpetuation, and additions were made as the stone passed from one generation to the next.

History has shown us that symbols of empire tend to proliferate as authority shrinks, and an example of this is the sarpech or turban ornament. In practice, the turban carried a special significance in that era being the prerogative of royalty and their nobles, and the gift of a turban was a mark of imperial esteem, a gracious honour selectively bestowed by the monarch. As the empire went into decline, the design of the sarpech became more elaborate, its use more widespread; doubtless there were loyalties to be bought and opposition to be placated. It was sadly noted by a contemporary historian that the grant of a sarpech was no longer regulated by the rank and dignity of the recipient.

From relatively simple beginnings—a bird's feather or kalgi swept back and weighted down with a pearl—the sarpech evolved until by the time of Shah Jehan it was intricately ornamented. The plume was now crafted from gold and gemstones and later still was added the sarpatti, a jewelled band across the forehead. In its most florid form the sarpech comprised the forehead band and a number of plumes, sometimes as many as five.

The glorious jewellery tradition of the Mughals did not disappear with the declining fortunes of the dynasty. Like so many other forms, miniature paintings for example, it spread to other areas, enriching regional characteristics and styles with the grandeur of its vision. Jewellery found a particularly fertile soil in Rajasthan, already renowned for the skill of its craftsmen, there to flourish in regions such as Jaipur, Bikaner and Jodhpur.

> *"A goddess? Or a rare peacock? Or a woman*
> *Decked with jewels?" asks my heart amazed.*

>   Tamil, from The Kural by Thiruvalluvar

Across South India, from the kingdoms of the Deccan sultans to the empire of Vijayanagara and the fiefdoms of the Malabar rajas, the jewellery repertoire was not only enormous but highly regionally varied. To attempt even a fair description of these riches would be to enumerate a catalogue of names and types, so let us concentrate on Tamil Nadu. Even here the repertoire is vast, its artistic expression catered to by the gold and gem mines of the south and the flourishing trade in gemstones.

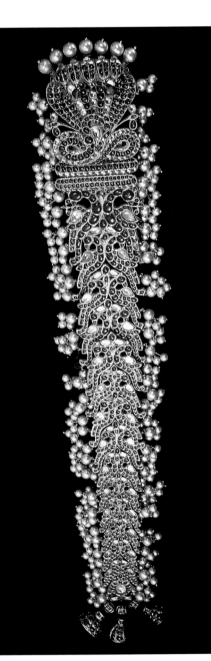

Gold was the predominant material of Tamil Nadu and its favourite gems, diamonds, rubies and pearls. The absence of multi-coloured gems was more than made up for by the very fine and highly skilled workmanship in gold. The descendants of the Chola artisans were masters of the repousse technique, that is, creating designs in relief by etching and hammering the gold from the reverse side. Such designs were often studded with precious stones. In stamp decoration work, patterned metal dies were used to form the impressions on gold.

Of the many ornaments in the area, three will give some idea of the jewellery, its artistry, its profound and constant connection with the world of nature and of the gods.

The jadanagam, an elaborate hair ornament, represents not only a high point in the jeweller's art but also visually encapsulates a number of concepts. Naga is snake, symbol of fertility and procreation, and the nagar crowns the ornament in the shape of a multiple-headed cobra. The rest of the jadanagam covers the braid, its snake-like form accentuating the fall of the hair and the shape of the plait underneath, ending in jaunty kunjalams or tassles. The triple strands of the hair that made up the plait were said to represent the three sacred rivers, Ganga, Jamuna and Saraswati. In its complete form the jadanagam would include a disc and a crescent, the sun and the moon. The ornament was an essential part of the shringar or decoration of the devadasi, the temple dancers.

Uniquely South Indian is the mangamalai, the mango necklace, whose origins go as far back as the Chola era. Long and heavy (in earlier times it would have gone down to the waist) it is a garland of mango-shaped pendants set with gems, usually rubies. The mango has many resonances: it is the sacred fruit of the gods ripened from a wish-fulfilling tree and stands for love and fertility. The characteristic fan-shaped pendant is fringed with pearls.

Tha tali represents the constancy of love in marriage and its antiquity is traced back to very early Tamil literature. From the day it is placed around her neck during her wedding ceremony, a woman never removes it unless parted by death. The word tali has been used interchangeably for the necklace as well as the pendant amulet that is such an important part of it, and it is worn throughout South India, including in non-Hindu communities. Fine and intricate versions of the tali are seen amongst the Nattukotai Chettiars of Tamil Nadu, a wealthy mercantile people. Here the distinctive pendant (athanam) is shaped like the four fingers of a hand, representing the four Vedas; this is surmounted by a depiction of the

Tali, Tamil Nadu, 20th cent. AD
The mangalsutra necklace, called tali in South India, is the enduring symbol of marriage. Its gold pendant too takes different shapes.

opp. Jadanagam, Tamil Nadu, ca. late 19th cent. AD
Hair braid ornament; the intricate gold design is studded with rubies and diamonds and fringed with pearls.

Mangamalai, Tamil Nadu, 19th cent. AD : A magnificent gold, ruby and pearl example of the "mango necklace", with its delicate mango motifs and characteristic fan-shaped pendant.

gods, very often Shiva and Parvati, the ideal union, or Lakshmi for prosperity. An important ceremony in the same community is the shashti poorthi; according to Hindu belief, a man's life span is 120 years and his sixtieth birthday celebrates its halfway mark. It is an occasion for celebration, an auspicious moment to wear the necklace known as rudraksha mala, also known as gaurishankaram or gaurisamgamam, made of the sacred beads. Its amulet box serves as a portable shrine, containing either the twin bead rudraksha symbolising the union of Shiva and Parvati, or vibhuti, the ashes from a consecrated fire, or a tiny Shiva linga.

In these great traditions of North and South we are reminded that jewellery is more than adornment or the sum of its parts and their value. The mastery of its craftsmen, nurtured by generations of inherited skills, served a cause beyond decoration. If the sarpech stood for temporal power, let us recall the emeralds engraved with holy words from the Qu'ran, objects of spiritual contemplation. Throughout India, such metaphors were part of the jewellery tradition, made richer by the amazing virtuosity of its craftsmen.

Anant, Bracelet, South India, 18th cent. AD
Rich with symbols, Anant (without end) represents the coiling and unending form of Anant or Shesh Nag, upon whose serpentine form rests Vishnu, Preserver of the Universe.
In the front of the picture is the lotus clasp, finely-worked in gold set with rubies and emeralds. Such a ceremonial bracelet, some believed, saved one from snake bite or the deadly effects of its poison.

four

FOLK AND TRIBAL JEWELLERY

"Myth is an experience which establishes kinship with everything around him."

Kamaladevi Chattopadhyay on tribal life

Myth is the foundation of the jewellery of rural and tribal peoples; it is not in the intent but in the material, therefore, that we should distinguish their jewellery from that of the classical tradition. There is a similar, perhaps greater, richness of belief and symbology; it is only that the expression takes different forms because of the relative lack of affluence. Gold is replaced by silver, precious stones by semi-precious ones; but now other

opp. Necklace, probably Orissa, ca. early 20th cent. AD
The necklace could have been used for ritual purposes or by a specially-designated person like a tribal priest. Notice the finely worked chain and the precision of the row of skulls (faces?) grinning out.

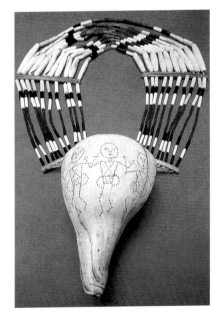

**Conch shell and bead necklace,
Nagaland, ca. early 19th cent. AD**
This man's necklace is from the Angami
tribe and is an ceremonial ornament.
The conch shell bears an interesting
motif of dancing figures.

materials enter, glass beads, cowrie shells, feathers, beetles, seeds, bone, dried flowers and grasses. As if to make up for their modest nature, they are worn in profusion, necklace upon necklace clasping the body from throat to breast; armlets and bangles from upper arm to wrist; multiple rings in ears pierced at life-enhancing points. Or the scale of the size changes, almost as if the ornament precedes the wearer to create a larger-than-life presence. Thus the giant hoop earrings that touch the shoulders, thus the nose rings so heavy that they must be supported with chains secured into the hair, or the anklets that appear like ornate cuffs for the legs.

No one single tradition predominates and even within areas and tribes there may be marked differences of observance. Among the bangle-loving Mudia Gonds, women of the Naitami clan are forbidden to wear bangles in the belief that if they do so their wrists will be encircled by snakes and their husbands will die. In Rajasthan, young married women add green glass bangles to their red ones in a shy, tender and unspoken acknowledgement of their pregnancy.

There are instances where the richness of so-called folk or tribal jewellery seems but another view of the opulence of mainstream tradition; equally, there are examples where stark minimalism dominates and where we must look beyond the surface to the meaning underneath. Jewellery extends beyond its conventional definition to include all forms of ornamentation such as festive or ritual head gear. Enough to say here that entire volumes could be written on this subject without exhausting it; of necessity, we can touch upon only a few areas.

It is another world-view we now enter where the forces of nature are experienced at first hand, making them far more immediate and felt. Wind, water, sky, tree and earth are the sources of spirits whose mysteries can never be fathomed by man, and who either bless him with good fortune or are malignant and must be warded off. Life hangs on the constant balance between the two and the power that either can have to influence happiness, prosperity and a bountiful harvest. Thus personal adornment has a magico-religious significance and its wearing the effect of a talisman.

The ga'u serves precisely this purpose, calling upon the mercy of benevolent

Baju-band, Rajasthan, ca. early 20th cent. AD
Silver baju-band (arm band) from Rajasthan, worn by the women of the Jat and Mina communities. The drawstring makes the ornament adjustable to the size of the wearer.

Peraks worn by Ladakhi women
Ladakhi women in their peraks,
hats studded with turquoise.
Ears and neck are adorned with
a profusion of seed pearls;
the box-like pendants are ga'us
containing talismanic charms.

forces to protect its wearer while trying to propitiate or ward off
those that are malignant. It is the charm box pendant worn in the
Buddhist areas of the Himalayas influenced by Tibet. The charms
within the box are vitalised through rituals and have the power to
deflect evil or sickness, which means that it must be in physical
contact with the body. It is quite usual to see people wearing a

number of ga'us simultaneously to take care of all eventualities. Ga'us come in all shapes and sizes, rectangular, octagonal, diamond-shaped, their surfaces often richly ornamented or studded with stones such as turquoise, agate or coral. From Ladakh in the west to Arunachal Pradesh in the east, ga'u pendants are a common sight, most often worn around the neck, sometimes pinned to hats or shawls.

The ladies of Ladakh who wear the ga'u also wear the perak, an open display of wealth and status. It is a head-dress, worn at its most glorious by rich matrons, often an heirloom piece passed from mother to daughter. It is interesting to see here a recurrence of the snake motif, for the perak looks like—and is meant to represent—a snake skin, harking back to the cobra whose hood sheltered Lord Buddha in meditation. Even so does the perak shelter its wearer against the harsh and icy winds of Ladakh, jutting over her brow like a cobra hood, tapering off like a snake skin at the back. Its entire ground is studded with turquoise stones of irregular shape and size, a hoard accumulated over years, maybe even a lifetime, which are glued or sewn on. The biggest and best stone is reserved for the front of the perak where it is clearly visible. Often ga'u boxes are secured on the crest of the perak in addition to being worn around the neck. Seed pearls are another gem of choice, being strung in multiple strands around the neck or draped over the ears and pinned to the hair.

East of Ladakh is the Himalayan state of Himachal Pradesh, part Buddhist, largely Hindu. If it is true that much of ancient Indian design remains in silver folk jewellery, then it is interesting to note the use of the chaunk, the original sisphul, worn on the crest of the head where, alas, it is not visible being covered by the head veil. Local ballads sing of a variety of

Kinnauri bride, Himachal Pradesh
Under her hat decorated with dried
flowers, the bride wears the tanaule
across her forehead, silver leaves
falling over her eyes.

opp. Aka girl, Arunachal Pradesh
Young maiden of the Aka tribe wears a
profusion of glass bead, stone and silver
necklaces, from one of which hangs the
ga'u or charm box. Her forehead is
encircled by the lenchhi, a band made
distinctive by the large silver disc in the
centre ornamented in repousse.

necklaces, bangles, anklets and earrings; and ornate
naths or nose rings, some so complicated and heavy
that they are chained to the hair and have to be lifted
to allow the woman to eat! Perhaps this is why in
one famous song a lover longs to be the nath on his
beloved's face so that he can kiss her lips...In the
high altitudes of Kinnaur women are profusely
adorned, and it is said that a bride may bear as much
as 15 kilos of silver on her wedding day. The local
blacksmith or domang doubles up as silversmith in
this once-remote area and one of his most delicate
creations is the bridal tanaule worn under the
woollen cap topped with dried flowers. Silver bands
go across the forehead, while cascading down to
frame and partly hide her face are shimmering pipal leaves in the
sheerest silver (pipala).

Over and over again, it is the richness of nature that provides much
of the inspiration and source for ornamentation whose vivid colours
reflect those of fruits and flowers. From nature's living kingdom of
animals and birds and serpents comes the personification of deities
and of honoured attributes. The Bison-horn Madias of Bastar take
their name from the horns they wear on their resplendent head-

dresses, a mark of vigour and youthful virility worn during the Gaur dances of courtship and marriage. Adorned with plumes and fringes of cowrie shells that cover the face and toss about as they dance, each head-dress is an heirloom passed proudly from father to son, and its loss or destruction causes terrible grief. The pastoral Todas of Tamil Nadu regard their buffalos as sacred; they are living deities gifted to them by the goddess Towkishy and they must be worshipped with strictly-observed rules and elaborate rituals. Buffalo ornaments were fashioned with as much care as those of the Todas themselves. In more than one region, the hornbill is a magic bird of great power, shining with courage and splendour; the right to wear its feathers is the privilege of only the brave.

We see this, for example, in Nagaland where, across 14 major tribes each with its own language, customs and traditions, the feathers of the hornbill feature almost everywhere in the state. Here is jewellery and ornamentation stunning in

**Neck band, Nagaland,
early 20th cent. AD**
Cast in the lost wax or cire perdue
method, the little rounds at the lower
end of this neck band could well be
representations of human heads.

**opp. Toda buffalo trappings,
Tamil Nadu, ca. early 20th cent. AD**
The sacred buffalos of the Todas were
worshipped through elaborate and secret
rituals, so it is not certain how this
ornament was placed on the animal.
Perhaps the cowrie shell discs were hung
over its horns, the silver chain slung low
around its neck.

its skilled use of a huge variety of material: beads, seeds, dyed animal
hair, cane, orchid stalks, animal horns, claws and bone, ivory and
cowrie shells, in addition to metals such as brass. These were
fashioned into all manner of adornments: necklaces, pendants,
breastplates, circlets, cuffs, belts, armlets and, of course, intricate
head-dresses, plumed with hornbill feathers, encrusted with the
shiny wings of beetles.

Male adornment is particularly notable, for jewellery and ornament
were once part of ceremonial dress worn on ritual occasions to

invoke the blessings of the crop spirits or those of the gods of war. Earrings and necklaces were worn by both men and women, but in ceremonial regalia, it was the men who were heavily decorated with these symbols of status and power. Wearing ornaments was a right that had to be earned through deeds of valour or merit such as the taking of heads or the giving of feasts. Head hunting (now long banned) was part of a community fertility rite. The human head represented the spirit inherent in the earth; to bring back a head or skull to

Nocte girl, Arunachal Pradesh
In her festive best, this girl from the Nocte tribe wears necklaces of coral, amber and silver with spacers of ivory, perhaps bone. Her coin necklace is, here as elsewhere, a mark of wealth.

the village after battle not only enhanced the standing of the warrior, it nourished the local crop. The right to wear hornbill feathers was won by those who had taken a head; they could also wear the head tally pendants or necklace, a graphic reminder of the number of heads they had captured. Feathers and pendants were thus highly-prized status symbols that publicly declared the valour and achievements of a man; they were the insignia of the warrior.

Clear across the country to the west is the area of Kutch in Gujarat, an arid scrubland which is a far cry from the verdant hills and lush vegetation of Nagaland. As if to compensate for that bleached landscape, Kutch is a repository of craft and colour, home to some of the most spectacular jewellery in India, a living tradition that is seen to this day. In all her finery, a woman might bear some three kilos or more of silver, but bear it she does, even in the remorseless heat of summer. In the Meghwal community of Banni, the jewellery is set against another kind of richness, that of embroidered garments whose colours are gem-like and precisely patterned, where inset mirror work flashes in the light of the sun. A Meghwal woman is a master of embroidey, just as her husband is skilled in leathercraft. An essential part of her jewellery repertoire is the varlo, a stiff and heavy torque of twisted silver wires. The varlo is worn along with a choker of beads—beadwork is another speciality—and many other necklaces. The intricate gold nose ring, the velado, is a sign of marriage and is worn only on special occasions. Ivory bangles (now more likely to be plastic) crowd her upper and lower arms.

As long as the traditions that created it remain, the jewellery of the people will continue to be made and worn. But seismic shifts are uprooting those traditions, and unhappily it will not be long before many of them disappear into museums, or, worse still, into oblivion.

Kutch woman, Gujarat
Meghwal woman from Banni, Kutch, wearing the varlo and the velado (silver wire necklace and gold nose ring). Note the silver earrings that cascade from the upper ear.

f i v e

CONTEMPORARY JEWELLERY

"I like to play with the three-dimensionality I see in surfaces."

Reena Thakur, award-winning designer

ewellery, with its wealth of meaning and symbol, has long been the unspoken language of the Indian people, equally dear to the hearts of those who wear diamonds as those who wear beads. Today it is acquiring a new vocabulary, a new dimension. In a country where many simultaneous levels co-exist, the bullock cart with the modem, the tug of tradition remains strong, articulated at

opp. Hansuli and bracelet, diamonds, Jaipur
A stunning Art Deco set executed in present-day Jaipur. Part of the elegant design emerges from the sophisticated juxtaposition of the baguette and rose-cut diamonds set in 18K gold and shimmering in the torque and its accompanying bracelet.

Ruby and diamond bracelet, Jaipur
This bracelet has an intriguing asymmetrical shape, reminiscent of the Art Deco pieces of the 1920s.
Square-cut rubies and round-cut diamonds on 18K gold accentuate the sinous curves of this jewel.

its most powerful during the wedding season. The wedding, of whichever community, region or economic level, continues to demand an age-old repertoire with its set pieces, most likely drawing on local jewellery skills known to a family for generations.

But—and especially in the big cities—there is a groundshift as new impulses attract the jewellery wearer to fresh areas. There are many reasons for this. Some of them have to do with the changing social fabric, whether we think of the gradual break-up of old family systems, the increased visibility of middle-class Indian women or the change in their costume from sari to skirt. Some reasons stem from a greater awareness of the global village, indeed, from globalisation itself, with all that it has come to mean in economic and cultural terms.

Earrings, 14K gold, diamonds, oxidised silver and Basra pearls, Jaipur
This lush display seems to show, in black, white and gold, control over form and exquisite setting.

History has shown, however, that Indians as a people are open to assimilation, with an uncanny capacity to absorb and internalise outside influences and transcreate them into a new and uniquely Indian expression. Before Shah Jehan ascended the Mughal throne, he saw portraits of James I of England in sweeping hats which featured jewelled aigrettes designed by Arnold Lulls, the 17th century Dutch designer. It was the inspiration he needed to commission the jewelled kalgi or turban feather in a distinctly Indian idiom, a favourite theme to this day. In similar vein, young designers today are adapting and innovating to create a new expression in jewellery.

From the late 19th century, Maharajas and their retinues began leisured excursions to Europe, carrying unused gemstones to set in the jewellery they would commission from the great houses of Paris. The designs travelled back, leading to the development of new styles, such as the Victorian with its ornate florals and leaves, its delicate designs elaborately expressed. Names like Cartier, Boucheron and Chaumet set the style for Indian royal jewellery and began a kind of exchange in designs, materials and techniques. The Art Deco movement of the 20th century borrowed heavily from exotic Oriental jewellery, especially Indian; in turn, the boldness of its designs, its angular symmetry and (paradoxically) the voluptuous elongated curves of some of its themes were eagerly adopted in India. As jewellery openly acknowledged its Western antecedents, the use of gemstones and the way they were cut and set changed. Lighter pieces, with bezelled stones in claw settings, became fashionable, an alternative to heavier traditional sets, yet still compatible with the flow and the drape of the sari.

Necklace and earrings, diamonds on oxidised silver, Jaipur
A floral extravaganza in true Victorian style; note the delicate use of small gems, which creates an almost ethereal effect.

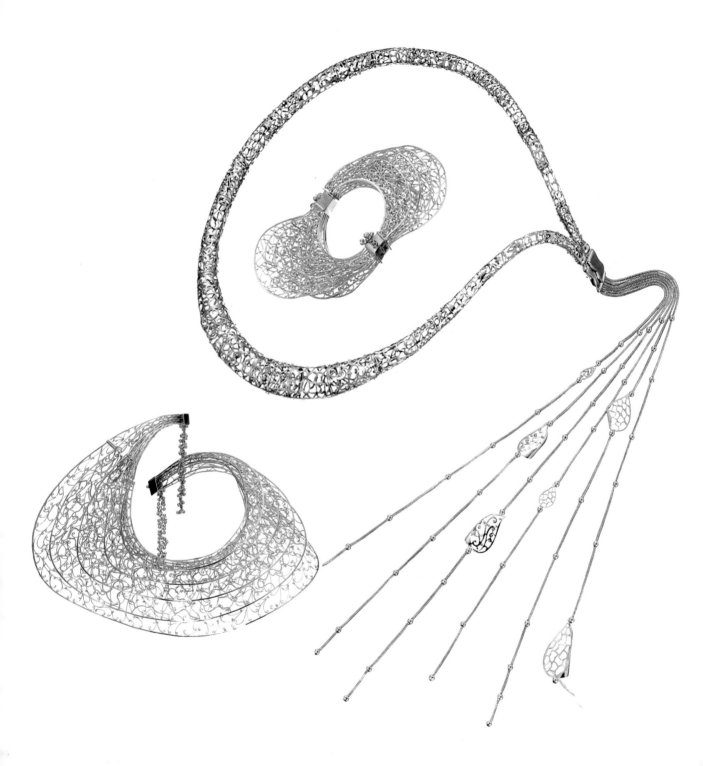

Slowly but surely, jewellery is evolving from its earlier concepts, from an investment and a language of symbols to a statement of its wearer's needs and her personal style. Those needs come from the demands of everyday life: functional jewellery that can be worn at the workplace, or is more appropriate for the western-style garments that she is likely to wear. It is part of her own perceptions about herself and her aspirations rather than an external social identifier of her roles as wife and mother. Even in this changing scenario, there are constants where the emotional bonding is so strong, the inherited connotations so resonant, that design experimentation would not be acceptable; rather, jewellery goes through a process of re-styling. This is seen in the tali or mangalsutra, for example, often adapted for lighter, easier wear; or the usage, by men and women, of significant gemstones for luck and prosperity. Thus development is taking place along many levels to open up new avenues.

**opp. "Wings of Fire" designer Sangeeta Dewan,
Winner of the Gold Virtuosi Award 2000**
This global competition, part sponsored by the World Gold Council, attracted over 1000 entries from 33 countries.

"I did the bracelet first. It has five wings each with a different pattern and technique, handcrafted filigree, wire work, cut work. It represents the coming together of different forms for a new way of life. The bracelet was fabricated from sheet metal but the same would have consumed too much gold for the necklace. So I worked with my craftsman— who's also an artist—and we made the necklace from gold wire but with the same look."

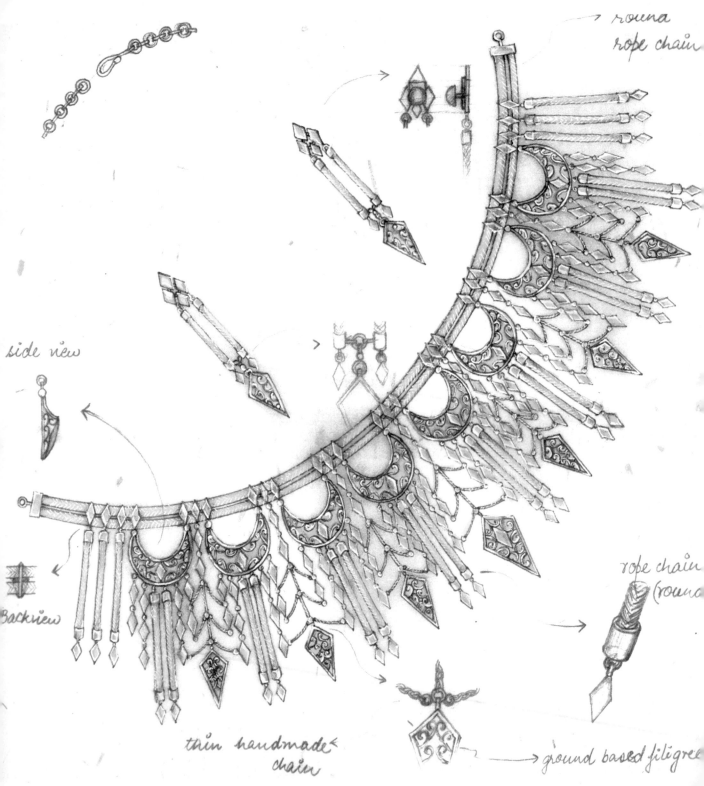

round
rope chain

side view

Backview

thin handmade
chain

rope chain
(round

ground based filigree

*"To me, jewellery is more about collectibles and less about a set
that you wear once and put away in the locker."*

Sangeeta Dewan, award-winning designer

In our admiration for jewellery as an art, we forget that it is, after all, also a business, providing employment to a labour force of two million skilled workers in the country. The export of gems and jewellery is the single largest foreign exchange earner in India, accounting for some 17% of total exports. The gamut covers cut and polished diamonds, coloured gemstones and pearls, gold and silver jewellery, as also fashion and costume jewellery. It is a vast machine whose thrust needs constant fuelling with new talent and new ideas to sustain its presence on the international scene. One of the most high-profile areas is that of design. It is an area where India has made a distinct mark thanks to institutes like NIFT (the National Institute for Fashion Technology) and others around the country. Such institutes provide the pool of vibrant young ideas from students who break barriers to create designs acclaimed all over the world. Many designs have won awards; and since they are not consciously "Indian", have found international acceptance.

opp. Page from the project portfolio of Deeksha Mishra
Such a project is part of the NIFT training and enables young designers to work to specific briefs with jewellers. This sketch, for a jeweller in Calicut catering to Mappila (Muslim) women, shows a design for a bridal collection which had to be innovative yet traditional. Persian-inspired motifs include half moons and thin, flat geometrical shapes linked by fine chains.

It is a different language these young designers speak. Acutely conscious of the weight of heritage, they are aware of the twin demands of tradition and modernity. They are highly sensitive to the marketplace, whether in India or elsewhere, because they work closely with jewellers and retailers. Vocabularies and needs differ from region to region; this, too, has to be taken into account. The ability to forecast and set design trends has to be balanced with the business and financial implications of such movements. They also work closely with the craftsmen; it is a two-way exchange where age-old techniques are adapted to new forms, and new skills are absorbed by the craftsmen, a platform for further innovation. Often, designers operate at two levels, one geared to the conservative buyer for whom jewellery retains its old value system, its significance of giving and taking, from which flow aspects like preferred materials (gold and diamonds, for example) and traditional designs. The second is that of the niches now being explored, many of them emerging from modern, big city lifestyles, such as the increase in the number of occasions when jewellery is gifted. Such niches may offer the opportunity to give expression to their inherent creativity in terms of abstract concepts and patterning.

Even at the first level of tradition, changes are taking place with the incorporation of new elements or a modification of material. These are design inputs often custom-tailored for a single buyer but which spark off a general interest. There is a greater use of materials like white gold or pink

"Autumn" (opp.) and "Concertina", Reena Thakur's Swarnanjali prize winners for the World Gold Council.

" 'Autumn' was inspired by the recurring idea of falling leaves which I froze in vibrant 22K gold. The leaves have an interesting three-dimensional curvature and I have textured different leaves with Indian techniques, such as filigree, Bengali rava, repousse and so on. It's fabricated so that the chain can be unlocked and the leaves slide out to be worn in many ways, as a brooch or hair accessory—it's really how you want to play with a piece of jewellery.

" 'Concertina' was visualised from the way the instrument is played, a motion from which different forms emerge. It is folded sheet metal, 22K gold which is softer to work with, on which I've used sand-blasting and chiselling. Again, this can be worn in many ways, the chain can be pulled out to make the piece flat like paper."

Peacock, designer Sangeeta Dewan, Swarnanjali prize winner.
The necklace is made of hinged units which can be unfastened to incorporate new units for a different look.

opp. Square bracelet and earrings, designer Pallavi Dudeja Foley
She has used the lines of barcodes to form these abstract graphics: in her own words "the designs of this collection clash with the perceptions of yesterday". The finish is in alternative stripes of glossy and matt 22K gold to create a sleek and modern look.

gold; there is gold that is rhodium-plated, even copper-plated, to give a variety of lustrous shades while still retaining the value of the metal. Young designers put forward the ensemble concept; an assembly of three necklaces of varying lengths, say, that can be worn together for grand occasions like weddings to look like a single large necklace of traditional appearance, or worn separately as smaller pieces. Detachable elements add versatility and change the look and colour of jewellery through interlocking devices that are delicately built in. Thus, hinged sections can be removed or added to change the length of a necklace; pendants double up as brooches; different pendants can be fitted on to a necklace to change its appearance and colour accentuation. Such innovations have been warmly welcomed; though, as most observers remark, they are not replacements for the standard repertoire but additions to it.

Again, there is a new trend towards branded jewellery which overrides regional variations. Over and above its design strengths, it is also a quality assurance to buyers, part of the increasing standardisation and hallmarking coming into the industry. But in the end, it is design and innovation that will differentiate in a competitive environment.

All these movements, the steady demand
for traditional sets, the new ideas now
expressed, draw heavily on the skills of
the sonar and his craftsmen while encouraging
him to develop new ones. The impetus of both
domestic and foreign markets have spurred the next
generation to return to an occupation once seen as unviable;
indeed, in Kolkata, a master goldsmith trains young workers in the
craft; whereas in places like Jaipur, a major jewellery centre, those
skills are kept alive by an unceasing flow of buyers. Many agencies
have worked together to sustain jewellery as a vibrant field both
artistically and commercially; the jewellery industry, the
Government, design schools as well as the burgeoning area of
fashion. Above all, it is the contribution of the sheer excellence of
the unknown, unseen artist whose perfection has been honed
over centuries.

GLOSSARY

Adiya, ariya	Literally, "rich"; a neck collar or choker with triangles dangling below in a spreading network.
Bajuband, bazuband	Armband, armlet, worn on the upper arm
Chudamani	Hair ornament worn on the crest of the head.
Ga'u	Charm box pendant of Tibetan origin, in wide use across the Buddhist regions of the Himalayas
Granulation	Technique of forming tiny gold spheres and adhering them to a gold surface.
Hansuli, hansli	Rigid necklace, torque, usually broader in front and tapering at the back.
Hath-phool	Literally, "flower for the hand". Linked ornament for the wrist, backs of the hands and fingers.
Jadanagam	Hair ornament for the plait.
Jhala, jhela	Narrow ornament going over the head to fall on either side. Often, earrings were attached to its lower ends.
Jhoomar	Head/hair ornament worn on one side of the forehead or over the ear.
Jhumka	Hanging ear ornament of a dome-like shape.
Kalgi	Feathered plume worn as a turban ornament, later also its jewelled form.
Karat	Term used to define the purity of gold; pure gold is 24K.
Karnaphool	Ear ornament or stud in the shape of a flower covering the ear lobe; which often had a jhumka dangling from it.
Kundala	Large earring in a circular shape.
Kundan	Soft gold, used in a special technique to encase gems.

Kunjalam	Tassle.
Mangalsutra	Marriage necklace.
Mangamalai	Necklace of mango motifs.
Meena	Enamel, the application of colours to a gold surface through repeated firings, the whole process of enamelling.
Mukut	Peaked crown for the head.
Nath	Nose ring, nose ornament.
Navratna	The nine auspicious gems associated with the planets.
Paizeb	Anklet, ankle ornament.
Perak	Unique ornamented head dress of Ladakhi women.
Rakhdi	Round hair ornament worn on the crest of the head.
Rudraksha mala	Necklace made of seeds or nuts from the utrasam tree (eleocarpus ganitrus); most often used as a rosary and in prayers.
Sarpatti	Turban ornament, usually hinged, tied across the forehead around the turban.
Sarpech	Turban ornament; originally any turban jewel, later often used to describe the jewelled or enamelled feather form.
Tali	South Indian marriage necklace with symbolic pendants.
Tanaule	Bridal ornament of Kinnaur, Himachal Pradesh.
Tinmaniya	Necklace of three gems
Varlo	Stiff heavy necklace of twisted silver wires worn by the Meghwal women of Kutch
Velado	Elaborate gold nose ring worn by the Meghwal women of Kutch.

Select Bibliography

Traditional Jewellery of India
   Oppi Untracht; Harry Abrams, New York, 1997

Dance of the Peacock: Jewellery Traditions of India
   Usha R. Bala Krishnan and Meera S. Kumar;
   India Book House, Bombay, 1999

A Golden Treasury, Jewellery from the Indian Subcontinent
   Susan Strong, Nima Smith and J. C. Harle;
   Mapin Publishing, Ahmedabad, 1988

Indian Jewellery
   M. L. Nigam; Roli Books, New Delhi, 1999

Treasury of the World: Jewelled Arts of India in the Age of the Mughals
   Manuel Keene and S. Kaoukji;
   Thames and Hudson, London, 2001

National Handicrafts and Handlooms Museum
   Jyotindra Jain and Aarti Aggarwala;
   Mapin Publishing, Ahmedabad, 1989

Crafts and Craftsmen in Traditional India
   M. K. Pal; Kanak Publications, New Delhi, 1978

ACKNOWLEDGEMENTS

For permission to photograph objects from their collections,
we would like to thank:

The National Museum, New Delhi; pages 1, 3, 5, 10 (both), 11 (both), 14, 16,
19, 22, 33, 49, 51, 52, 53, 58, 59, 61,63, 65
with special thanks to Mrs. Rita Devi Sharma, Keeper, for her assistance.

Modi's The Ganpati Gems and Arts, Jaipur; pages 2, 18, 24, 35, 40 to 46, 60,
78, 80: photographer, Mahesh Hariani.

Bhuramal Rajmal Surana, Jaipur; pages 13 (both), 54, 55, 56, 81, 83:
photographer, Jitendra Olaniya.

The Heritage Jewels, Jaipur; pages 6, 26, 29, 57: photographer, Jitendra Olaniya.

Thanks also to following persons and institutions for their generous assistance:

At NIFT, Mr. Jatin Bhatt and Mr. Arvind Merchant; at Punjab Jewellers, Karol Bagh,
New Delhi, Mr Sanjiv Verma; designers Sangeeta Dewan, Reena Thakur and
Pallavi Dudeja Foley, all of whom provided valuable inputs for Chapter 5.

Picture Credits

For permission to use images from their collections, we would like to thank:

The National Handicrafts and Handlooms Museum (Crafts Museum), New Delhi pages 30, 31, 62, 64, 66, 68, 69, 74, 75.

The National Museum, New Delhi, Dancing Girl, page 8.

The Government Museum, Mathura, Mother Goddess, page 9.

The Patna Museum, Patna, Tara, page 12; Lokanatha, page 15; Nayika from Deogarh, page 48.

The Trustees, Chhatrapati Shivaji Maharaj Vastu Sanghralaya, formerly Prince of Wales Museum of Western India, Mumbai, Lady being offered wine, page 50.

C.L. Bharany, pictures by Avinash Pasricha courtesy the Enamelist Society, pages 20 and 37.

The Diamond Information Centre, pages 38 and 39.

Indiapicture: Amandeep Singh Kalra, page 70; B.P.S.Walia, page 72; Ashok Nath, pages 73 and 76; Maryam Reshi, page 77.

Sangeeta Dewan, page 84.

NIFT (National Instt. of Fashion Technology), page 86 .

World Gold Council, pages 88, 89, 90.

Tanishq, page 91.